The Magical Garden

By Janice Lee

Illustrated by John Huang

Janice Lee

The Magical Garden

Reading Roots

First Edition

Softcover ISBN: 978-1-7781672-2-5
Hardcover ISBN: 978-1-7781672-1-8
Electronic ISBN: 978-1-7781672-2-5

Illustrated by John Huang

To my grandparents, with love.

The bell chimed as the clock struck noon. Everyone looked at the garden as the ringing sound travelled to their ears.

"The fruit growing festival is about to begin!", said Grandma Edna.

"This year, we chose four children to join the festival to learn how to grow fruits."

The children gathered at the garden and lined up from left to right: Adrian, Bella, Duan and Charite.

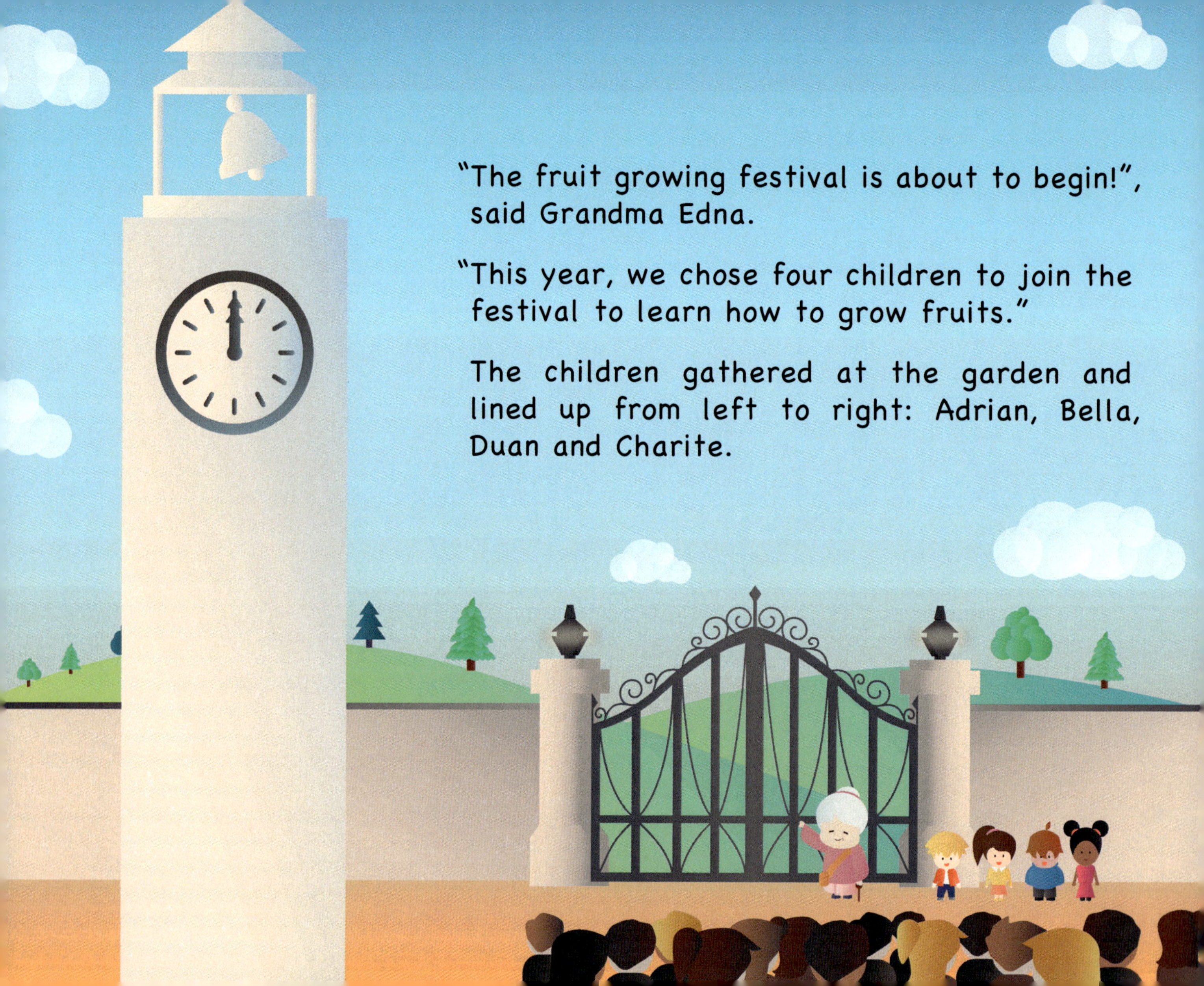

As the gate to the garden opened, the children jumped up and down with excitement.

The children followed Grandma, marching along with the click clack sounds of her cane hitting the ground.

Click clack click clack...Grandma slowed down and pointed at a hill with no trees. The children looked at each other in confusion as they stood in front of the hill.

"I want each of you to grow a fruit you love.", said Grandma.

Adrian exclaimed, "I want to grow apples!".

Bella shouted, "Blueberries!".

Charite uttered, "Cantaloupe!".

Duan mumbled, "Durian."

Each child planted their seeds into the empty land.

Days passed and Adrian's plant grew into a tree full of apples. Adrian jumped up and down with excitement. Bella, Charite and Duan were sad because their plants had no fruit.

Bella asked, "Why are there no blueberries?"

Grandma calmly responded, "Patience child, growing fruit is a process and great things take time. Do not compare, just keep watering and your plant will soon grow blueberries."

Days passed and Bella's plant was full of blueberries. Duan's tree was full of durians.

Duan held the durian in his hand as he watched Bella and Adrian enjoy their fruits.

"What is that smell?", shouted Adrian and Bella.

Duan was embarrassed because of the smell of the durians.

Grandma said, "Some people like durian, and some people don't like durian. Whether they like it or not, it should not change your love for durian."

Cries from afar caught
Grandma's attention.

Charite's cantaloupe plant
was small with no fruit.

She cried for help.

Grandma calmly said, "My child, the weather is not good for growing cantaloupe. Are there are any other fruits you want to grow?"

Charite shouted, "I am going to grow my second favourite fruit: cherries!".

Charite started to plant the cherry seed. The children all worked together to help Charite grow cherries.

Days passed and Charite's tree started to grow cherries.

"You all learned to grow fruits and helped each other! Now it's time to pick the fruits." said Grandma.

The children carried the basket of fruits and followed Grandma. The sound of grandma's cane hitting the ground going click clack click clack...

Grandma led the children out of the garden. She smiled and waved bye to the children. She closed the gate, ending the fruit growing festival.

Manufactured by Amazon.ca
Bolton, ON

26519062R00017